POWER
YESTERDAY ● TODAY ● TOMORROW

ENERGY
FROM
THE WIND
GENERATING POWER WITH WIND TURBINES

by Ruth Owen

PowerKiDS
press
New York

Published in 2013 by The Rosen Publishing Group, Inc.
29 East 21st Street, New York, NY 10010

Produced for Rosen by Ruby Tuesday Books Ltd
Editor for Ruby Tuesday Books Ltd: Mark J. Sachner
US Editor: Sara Antill
Designer: Emma Randall
Consultant: Kenneth A. Walz, Ph.D.; K-12 Energy Education Program; University of Wisconsin-Stevens Point

Library of Congress Cataloging-in-Publication Data

Owen, Ruth, 1967–
 Energy from the wind : generating power with wind turbines / by Ruth Owen.
   p. cm. — (Power: yesterday, today, tomorrow)
Includes index.
ISBN 978-1-4777-0271-0 (library binding) — ISBN 978-1-4777-0281-9 (pbk.) — ISBN 978-1-4777-0282-6 (6-pack)
1. Wind power—Juvenile literature. 2. Wind turbines—Juvenile literature. I. Title.
TJ820.O947 2013
621.31'2136—dc23

                                         2012034681

Manufactured in the United States of America

CPSIA Compliance Information: Batch #W13PK7: For Further Information contact Rosen Publishing, New York, New York at 1-800-237-9932

CONTENTS

Wind Power

Some call **wind turbines** colossal, sculpture-like, wonders of green technology. Others say they are ugly eyesores that ruin natural landscapes. Are they noisy killers of wildlife, or one of the ways to save our planet for the future? Wherever in the world they are built, wind turbines have their critics and their supporters.

As tall as 20-story buildings with **blades** as long as a football field, wind turbines are giant windmills that are used to generate electricity. In 2011, wind turbines produced about 3 percent of the electricity generated in the United States. That's enough to supply the needs of 10 million homes. There is, however, potential to produce much, much more.

Worldwide, scientists, engineers, and environmental activists are working to improve wind technology and persuade people that more wind power is needed. This is important work. Every day, more and more electricity is used to run our modern world. Unfortunately, the main fuels we currently use to produce electricity are running out. Their use is also damaging Earth.

Generating electricity with wind power produces no damaging air **pollution**. Also, this type of energy is **renewable**, which means it will never run out!

These offshore wind turbines have been built in the ocean just off the coast of Copenhagen, Denmark

These dairy cows share their pasture with wind turbines that are generating electricity.

FAST FACT

If all the wind power available on land in the United States could be harnessed, it would produce 10 times the amount of electricity needed by the nation. Even more electricity would become available if all the offshore wind power was also harnessed.

Generating Electricity

How many things have you touched, used, and enjoyed today that would not exist without electricity to run them, or power the factories where they are produced? Some of these things include sneakers, MP3 players, TVs, curling irons, iPads, cell phones, and soda cans.

It's easy to take electricity for granted without thinking about how it is generated, or what source of power is used to make it.

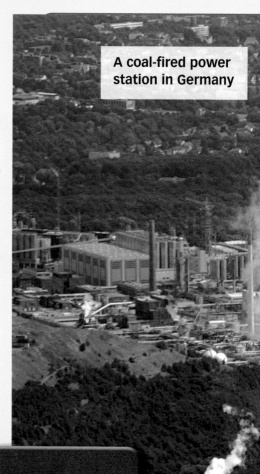

A coal-fired power station in Germany

Most electricity is generated in power stations. In the United States, around 70 percent of the electricity produced each year is made using coal or **natural gas**. At a coal-fired power station, coal is burned inside huge boilers that heat water to such a high temperature that it becomes steam. Then the steam is used to spin giant turbines. The turbines power **generators**, which produce electricity.

Coal and gas have been major sources of fuel for electricity production for decades. Today, however, that has to change. Burning these fuels is harming the planet. What's more, supplies of these fuels, buried deep inside Earth, are running out—fast!

FAST FACT

*In 2011, just 13 percent of the electricity generated in the United States came from environmentally-friendly, renewable power sources. These included hydropower, which uses fast-moving water to spin a power station's turbines, and solar power, which uses the Sun's energy to heat water and make steam inside a power station or to generate electricity inside devices called **solar cells**.*

Electricity is essential to our modern lives. We use it 24 hours a day to have fun, to communicate and do business, and to manufacture goods in factories.

The Trouble with Fossil Fuels

Coal, natural gas, and oil are known as **fossil fuels**. Over millions of years, these fuels formed underground from the remains of ancient plants and animals. Fossil fuels are **nonrenewable** because we can't make any more.

Even if we could create more fossil fuels, it wouldn't be wise. When fossil fuels are burned, gases such as carbon dioxide, methane, and nitrous oxide are released into Earth's **atmosphere**. Known as **greenhouse gases**, these gases trap the Sun's heat on Earth, just as a greenhouse traps heat inside.

Coal is being extracted from the ground at this surface coal mine in Gillette, Wyoming. The coal is then carried on a conveyor belt to a nearby coal-fired electricity power station.

We need heat and light on Earth to survive, but too much heat is a problem. Burning fossil fuels is causing a gradual increase in Earth's temperatures that most scientists agree is leading to **climate change**.

An increase in temperatures will cause ocean levels to rise, because water expands when it is heated. This could lead to flooding in low-lying coastal places. Ice at the North and South poles will also melt. In some places, the climate could become so hot and dry that water supplies will dry up and people will not be able to grow crops.

FAST FACT

Fossil fuels formed when plants and animals died and their remains settled on the ocean floor and at the bottom of swamps.

Over time, the remains were buried by layers of soil or water.

Heat and pressure turned the remains to oil, natural gas, and coal that we extract from deep underground.

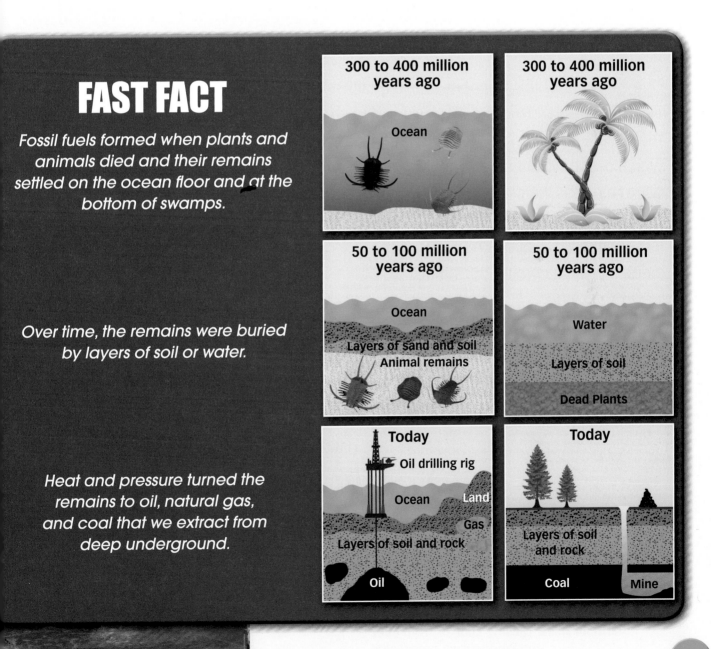

How Wind Works

You probably feel or see wind in action every day of your life. But what exactly is wind?

Wind is air that is moving around. As the Sun warms up our planet, the planet's surface absorbs heat at different rates. This is because there are many variations in the Earth's surface, from high mountains, to deep valleys, and wide, flat oceans. The difference in heat absorption means the air is warmer in some places and cooler in others. It's these differences in air temperature that cause air to move.

One example of this happens at the beach. During the day, the air above the land warms up more quickly than the air above the ocean. The warm air expands and becomes less dense, which causes it to rise. As the lighter warm air rises, heavier, cool air from over the water rushes into the space left behind. We feel this movement of air as a breeze coming off the ocean.

Day and night, all over the world, the warming and cooling of air causes air to move around and wind to happen.

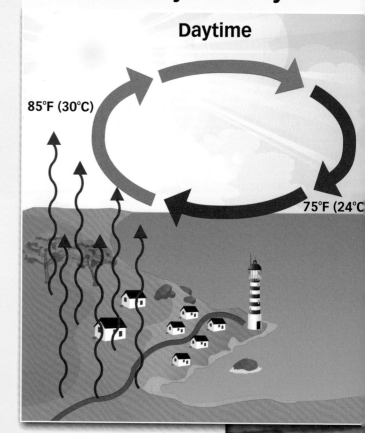

The Daily Wind Cycle

Daytime

85°F (30°C)

75°F (24°C)

During the day, warm air over land rises, causing cold air to take its place (right). At night this process is reversed. Air above the ocean is warmer than on land. This warm air rises, causing cool air from over the land to rush out to sea.

A windsurfer uses moving air, or wind, to skim over the water's surface.

FAST FACT

Antarctica is the coldest, driest, windiest continent on Earth. In places, winds can blow at over 200 miles per hour (322 km/h). While no one permanently lives in Antarctica, thousands of scientists visit each year. Wind turbines are being used to harness Antarctica's fierce winds to provide power to the research stations where the scientists live and work.

From Ancient Sailboats to Electricity

People have harnessed the wind's energy since earliest recorded history.

Over 5,000 years ago, the ancient Egyptians used wind power to travel and transport goods along the Nile River in sailboats. In time, people realized that when sails were attached to a structure on land, the turning of the sails created mechanical energy that could be used to drive machinery. The windmill was born!

The wind-powered sails of traditional windmills turned an axle, which then drove any combination of cogs and wheels in other machines. Windmills were used for grinding grain into flour, cutting timber in sawmills, and powering machinery that pumped water. When electricity came into use, windmills were adapted to run generators that could supply small quantities of electricity to farms and rural homes.

Eventually, burning fossil fuels became the preferred way of generating large quantities of electricity. In the 1980s and 1990s, however, the drive to use renewable energy and protect the environment led to a revival in using windmills to produce electricity. Wind power, a form of energy that had been used since ancient times, was back!

These sailboats on the Nile River in Egypt are powered by wind in the same way as boats that sailed the river 5,000 years ago.

Sails

Sails

These traditional windmills from Denmark (left) and the United Kingdom (above) were both built in the 1800s.

Charles F. Brush's giant wind turbine was built to generate electricity. Note the size of the person in the bottom of the picture!

FAST FACT

In the late 1880s, an American inventor named Charles F. Brush built a giant wind turbine in his backyard. The machine's rotor had a diameter of 56 feet (17 m). Brush's wind turbine produced enough electricity to power over 350 lights and a number of motors in his home.

Electricity from Wind

Most wind turbines have three huge blades that are mounted on a drive shaft. Just like blowing on a pinwheel, when the wind catches the turbine's blades, they begin to spin.

As the blades spin, they turn the drive shaft, which is inside a box called the **nacelle**. Inside the nacelle is the turbine's generator. As the drive shaft turns, it spins the generator, which then produces electricity.

The turbine's weather station monitors the wind's speed and direction. It sends this information to the turbine's computer, which then turns the nacelle and blades so they are always facing into the wind to capture the most energy.

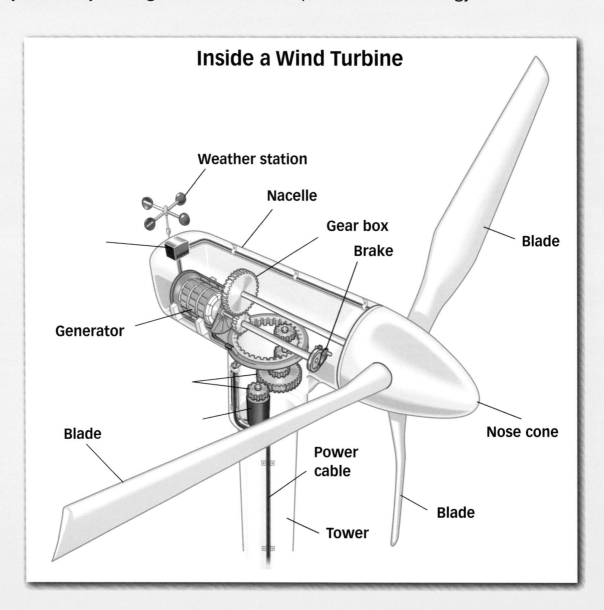

Inside a Wind Turbine

Weather station

Nacelle

Gear box

Brake

Blade

Generator

Blade

Nose cone

Power cable

Blade

Tower

The electricity that's generated by the wind turbine flows down a power cable inside the tower. The cable then carries the electricity underground to wherever it is needed.

It may cost around $1.5 million to manufacture and install a large wind turbine (and that doesn't include buying the land or laying the power lines). The turbine produces electricity using a free source of energy, however, and no harmful greenhouse gases are created!

FAST FACT

A very large wind turbine at a site with regular, powerful winds could produce enough electricity in a year to power over 1,000 homes.

When seen up close, wind turbines are huge! This five-year-old child is standing where the turbine's nose cone will be fitted.

A wind turbine's blades and nacelle can turn 360 degrees to always face in the best direction for catching wind.

Windmills, Egg Beaters, and the Trouble with Turbines

There are two main types of wind turbines—horizontal-axis turbines, which look like giant windmills, and vertical-axis turbines, which sometimes look like giant egg beaters!

The most commonly used design today is the horizontal-axis turbine, which has two, three, or four blades on a tall tower. These turbines can be 20 stories tall and have blades that are 200 feet (61 m) long. The blades are mounted high up to catch fast-moving winds that are not as turbulent as winds closer to the ground.

The blades of vertical-axis turbines extend from the top to the bottom of the structure. These turbines are usually around 100 feet (30 m) tall. Invented in the 1930s, the two-bladed egg beater design is called a Darrieus wind turbine, after its inventor, a French engineer named Georges Darrieus.

Many people love to see turbines dotting the countryside. While these huge and unusual structures change the natural look of the landscape, these people feel it's a change worth making. Other people feel that turbines are ugly. They believe rural areas and coastlines should be left unspoiled, and alternative ways to make electricity be found.

FAST FACT

Homeowners in windy places who want to use environmentally-friendly electricity can install a small wind turbine on their house. Small turbines can also be built in remote villages or on ranches where people cannot connect to a larger **electrical power grid**. *A wind turbine can even be used to make electricity for a trailer home or boat!*

A small wind turbine and solar panels producing "green" electricity on the roof of a trailer home

Darrieus wind turbines

It's Tough at the Top!

When it comes to maintaining and repairing wind turbines, all the important stuff has to happen high up. Very high up indeed!

Wind turbine technicians are highly skilled people who help construct new wind turbines. They also carry out regular maintenance checks and repair the turbines when they develop problems. Sometimes technicians might have to collect data to be used in new research.

Wind turbine technicians must have an in-depth knowledge of every aspect of how the wind turbine works. They also have to be able to work in the open air, 300 feet (91 m) above the ground, without getting dizzy!

A typical day begins with a long climb straight up a 20-story ladder inside the turbine's tower. For safety, technicians operate a buddy system and always work in pairs. They also use ropes and harnesses to keep them attached to the wind turbine, much like the gear rock climbers use. At the top of the ladder, it's out into the open air to begin work. When all the tasks are completed, there's another long climb back down the ladder to Earth!

Wind turbine technician Ross Kennedy gets to work on a turbine in Scotland. Not only is Ross high off the ground, but the nacelle continually moves as it searches for the best position to catch wind.

Wind Farms

A **wind farm** is a group of wind turbines all placed in one location. There may be hundreds of individual turbines on a large wind farm.

Most large wind farms produce electricity that goes to the country's electrical power grid. While all the electricity generated goes to the same place, the turbines on a wind farm are not connected. Each one operates independently, so a wind farm is like having hundreds of individual power stations.

Offshore wind farms are built in shallow coastal waters. The wind over the ocean is usually faster and stronger than on land. There are also no obstacles, such as trees, buildings, or mountains, to slow it down or create turbulence.

In order to take advantage of higher, stronger ocean winds, offshore wind turbines are much larger and taller than land turbines. They also have to be strong enough to withstand powerful waves. The towers of offshore turbines stand in the ocean and are buried in the seabed.

The electricity that's generated at offshore wind farms flows through undersea cables and is then supplied to the electrical power grid on land.

Wind turbines under construction at a wind farm

FAST FACT

Many wind farms are owned by business people who produce electricity and then sell it to large electricity companies that supply power to homes and businesses.

C-Power

These massive turbines at the Thornton Bank offshore wind farm, off the coast of Belgium, stand 600 feet (184 m) above the seabed!

Finding Windy Places

The wind turbines on a wind farm must produce as much electricity as possible to pay back the expense of buying and installing all the equipment. Therefore, choosing the right place to build the farm is very important.

Companies building wind farms will record data about a potential site's wind speed and direction for at least a year. A good site will have consistent wind at average speeds of at least 10 miles per hour (16 km/h).

Good places to build wind farms include open plains and smooth hills with no windbreaks, such as trees. Gaps, or passes, between mountains also work well because wind is forced to flow through a narrow area.

At the Tehachapi Pass wind farm in California, the summer months are the windiest months. The extremely hot summer weather in Southern California heats the air above the Mojave Desert. The hot air rises and causes cool air from over the Pacific Ocean to rush through the mountain pass between the Tehachapi Mountains to get to the desert. The wind farm is perfectly positioned in the mountain pass to take advantage of these winds.

FAST FACT

The windy summer months are when the Tehachapi Pass wind farm generates the most electricity. This perfectly suits the electricity needs of the region it supplies. In California, people use more electricity in the summer because they are running air conditioning systems.

The Tehachapi Pass wind farm in California has been operating since the 1980s. These are some of the older wind turbines still at work on the farm.

An aerial view of the Tehachapi Pass wind farm in California

Wind Power Gets Supersized

In the future, the wind turbines that generate our electricity could be getting a lot bigger!

In 2012, the German engineering and electronics company Siemens produced the world's longest wind turbine blades. The B75 rotor blades are designed for use on offshore wind turbines.

Each supersized blade is 246 feet (75 m) long. That's almost as long as the wingspan of an Airbus A380, the largest passenger plane in the world.

A giant B75 wind turbine blade

o make the blades, Siemens used a ew process that enables each blade to e made in a single piece. The blade is nade from glass fiber-reinforced epoxy esin and balsa wood. This material is oured into a giant mold, and then it ets. The blade, therefore, has no seams r joints, which makes it extremely trong with no weak points. That's a ood thing, because the blades will have o withstand being hit by the energy of 00 tons (181 t) of air every second.

This diagram shows the size of the B75 wind turbine blades in comparison with an A380 Airbus.

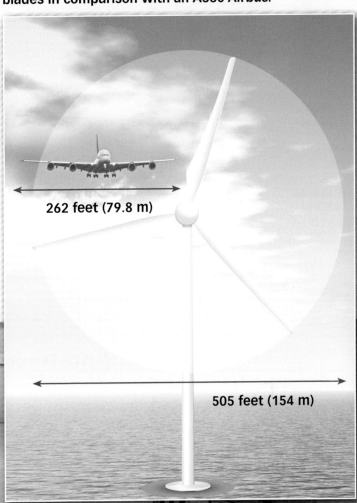

262 feet (79.8 m)

505 feet (154 m)

FAST FACT

As technology has improved, so has the size of wind turbines and the amount of power they can produce. Electricity is measured in small units of power called watts. The first wind turbines had 16-foot-(5 m) long blades, and produced around 30,000 watts (or 30 kilowatts) of electricity. Today's largest, most advanced turbines can produce 6 million watts (or 6 megawatts) of power.

Is Wind Power Perfect Power?

To combat climate change, we need to generate electricity in a way that doesn't produce greenhouse gases. We also need to produce our power with an energy source that is renewable. Making electricity with wind energy puts a check mark next to both of these boxes!

Wind power is green, and it's renewable. Does it have other benefits, too? And are there any downsides to using this type of energy?

Wind Power Pros

✔ *Each individual wind turbine requires a very small footprint of land. This means wind turbines can be built on fields that are used for farming and grazing animals. This gives the land several uses.*

✔ *Wind farm companies will pay farmers rent to use their land as a place to install wind turbines. This gives farmers an extra way to earn income. It may also keep a landowner from selling off fields to companies who will build houses or factories in these green places.*

✔ *Traditional fossil-fueled power stations use huge quantities of water to produce electricity. No water is used in the generation of electricity using wind power.*

✔ *Many countries do not have their own stocks of fossil fuels, or they have insufficient stocks, so they have to buy fuel from other countries. These nations may be able to produce their own electricity using wind power.*

✔ *Manufacturing the many different parts used in wind turbines creates jobs.*

✔ *Energy from the wind is completely free to use!*

Wind Power Cons

 Some designs of wind turbines are responsible for the deaths of many birds and bats when the animals fly into the blades. Wind turbine designers are working to make turbines safer. For example, today's turbine blades move slower and are much higher in the air, so they do not interfere with the flight paths of many types of birds. Wind turbines are also getting larger and more powerful. This means fewer are needed, and those that are built are easier for animals to see.

Day or night, energy from the wind can be used to generate electricity.

X Wind farms require the building of roads to allow people access to the turbines. Also, natural habitats may be disturbed by the laying of power cables underground from the turbines to the electrical power grid.

X Manufacturing the wind turbines themselves and making products such as concrete that are used in their installation uses lots of energy and water.

X The building of offshore wind turbines may disturb fish and other ocean animals.

X Some people who live near wind turbines are disturbed by the sound of the blades turning.

X Wind turbines are very large structures, and many people do not like the way they change the appearance of natural landscapes.

A Bright and Breezy Future?

Today, we can use energy from the wind to power a single home using a small wind turbine, or generate electricity for hundreds of thousands of homes on a wind farm.

Wind energy has been around since our planet first formed. We've gotten very good at harnessing its power, but the technology to use it to its full potential is still relatively young. Worldwide, thousands of people in the wind power industry are developing new technologies and working to find ways to harness more power from the wind.

FAST FACT

To make the same amount of electricity in a coal-fired power station that a 1-megawatt wind turbine will produce in 20 years, it would require the burning of about 29,000 tons (26,000 t) of coal and the use of about 60 million gallons (227 million l) of water!

A truck on its way to a new wind farm carrying a blade for a wind turbine

Our world's need for electricity isn't going to go away. Wind offers us an excellent opportunity for producing power in a pollution-free, **sustainable** way. In fact, with more development of this industry, the environmental group Greenpeace estimates that wind power could supply around 34 percent of the entire world's electricity needs by the year 2050.

One thing is certain. As long as the Sun keeps shining and warming the air on Earth, there will always be plenty of wind. It's up to us to make use of it!

The Dubai World Trade Centre, in the United Arab Emirates, has wind turbines for generating electricity incorporated into the building's stunning design.

Glossary

atmosphere (AT-muh-sfeer)
The layer of gases surrounding a planet, moon, or star.

blade (BLAYD)
A long, paddle-like or armlike part of a wind turbine that catches the wind and turns.

climate change (KLY-mut CHAYNJ)
The gradual change in temperatures on Earth. For example, the current warming of temperatures caused by a buildup of greenhouse gases in the atmosphere.

electrical power grid
(ih-LEK-trih-kul POW-er GRID)
A system of power lines that connects homes and other buildings to electrical power stations.

fossil fuels (FO-sul FYOOLZ)
Fuels that formed over millions of years from the remains of plants and animals. Oil, natural gas, and coal are all fossil fuels.

generator (JEH-neh-ray-tur)
A machine that turns mechanical energy, for example the spinning of a turbine, into electrical energy.

greenhouse gases
(GREEN-hows GAS-ez)
Gases such as carbon dioxide, methane, and nitrous oxide that occur naturally and are also released into Earth's atmosphere when fossil fuels are burned.

nacelle (nuh-SEL)
The boxlike structure at the top of a wind turbine that contains the generator and other pieces of machinery and equipment.

natural gas (NA-chuh-rul GAS)
A fossil fuel that formed underground over millions of years. It is piped to homes and businesses to be used as a source of energy.

nonrenewable (non-ree-NOO-uh-bul)
A resource, such as coal, that cannot be renewed once it is used.

ollution (puh-LOO-shun)
il, garbage, chemicals, or gases that
ave escaped into water, air, or onto
nd and are causing damage.

enewable (ree-NOO-uh-bul)
resource that can be produced again
nd again and will not run out.

olar cell (SOH-ler SEL)
device made from silicon and
hemicals that absorbs sunlight and
enerates electricity.

sustainable (suh-STAY-nuh-bel)
Using resources in a way that can
continue into the future without causing
damage to the environment.

wind farm (WIND FAHRM)
A collection of wind turbines in one
location. A wind farm may have
hundreds of wind turbines spread
over thousands of acres (ha).

wind turbine (WIND TER-byn)
A machine, like a windmill, that uses
blades to catch the wind and turn
a drive shaft, which spins a generator
that produces electricity.

WEBSITES

Due to the changing nature of Internet links, PowerKids Press has
developed an online list of websites related to the subject of this book.
This site is updated regularly. Please use this link to access the list:

www.powerkidslinks.com/pytt/wind/

Read More

Benduhn, Tea. *Wind Power*. Energy for Today. New York: Gareth Stevens, 2009.

Kamkwamba, William. *The Boy Who Harnessed the Wind*. New York: Dial Books for Young Readers, 2012.

Spilsbury, Richard, and Louise Spilsbury. *Wind Power*. Let's Discuss Energy Resources. New York: PowerKids Press, 2012.

Index